KON-TIKI
AND I

KON-TIKI AND I

Illustrations with
text begun on the Pacific
on board the raft "Kon-Tiki"
and completed at
"Solbakken" in Borre.

BY ERIK HESSELBERG

Prentice-Hall, Inc.
Englewood Cliffs, New Jersey

KON-TIKI AND I
by Erik Hesselberg
© 1970 by Erik Hesselberg

Library of Congress Catalog Card Number: 73-92381

Printed in the United States of America • *J*

13–516716–7

Prentice-Hall International, Inc., London
Prentice-Hall of Australia, Pty. Ltd., Sydney
Prentice-Hall of Canada, Ltd., Toronto
Prentice-Hall of India Private Ltd., New Delhi
Prentice-Hall of Japan, Inc., Tokyo

Introduction

In 1947, six men set out to cross the Pacific Ocean from Peru to Polynesia—4300 miles of open ocean—on a raft! This was the famous Kon-Tiki expedition.

These men were attempting to prove that the people of Polynesia had originally come from Peru by crossing the ocean on a raft, and led by a man called Kon-Tiki. Since no one would believe that it was possible to make such a voyage, these six decided to show that it was. They built a raft similar to the primitive Peruvian ones and, with no modern equipment except for a small radio, with no method of steering their craft and only the wind and current to take them, succeeded in making the crossing!

Erik Hesselberg, the only licensed seaman on board, was the navigator of the raft. He is also an accomplished artist and, as he tells it, he "brought along a bottle of Chinese ink and sketched a little every day on the raft in order to have a record for my friends and family."

Kon-Tiki and I is Erik Hesselberg's own story of this incredible voyage, accompanied by the sketches he made while he was on it.

A Little Story About Myself

The sea was not all around me in the beginning of my life, just on one side but very near. The small ports of Brevik and Larvik in Norway became the promising gates to horizons and adventures. At the age of seventeen, I was a deckboy on board a ship bound for Trinidad. A seaman's life was pretty hard at that time, four hours watch and four hours sleep, but I enjoyed it. Five years later I had been twice around the world and had a navigation license in my pocket. But I was too fond of life on land to continue on the sea. Because I liked to paint and draw, I decided to become a painter. I knew by now that I was not meant for any professional career. Somehow as an artist I succeeded in keeping my life on the European continent nearly free. The little I earned was enough to live on. After the Kon-Tiki expedition I lived again on a boat for about eleven years mostly near Provence, Corsica, and Italy. I was painting, writing, and composing music. After that I did some engravings and forms in a special kind of concrete. Among them is Picasso's huge statue of "Sylvette" in New York City. So, when you look at her you see a little bit of me too.

Erik Hesselberg

Dedicated to my wife
Liss
who had to sit at home
and mind the child
Anne Karin
while I was having
        strange experiences.

My family I left behind, and "Solbakken" (which means the sunhill). "Solbakken" was the name of the house we lived in. It stands close to the Borre Church and looks like this.

Borre itself is just a little village in South Norway. I left it; Pius, my noble cat; Casa Nova, the cock; and the five hens: Sofie, Amalie, Christine, Agate, and Gerd. Gerd was the youngest and was always being pecked and hustled by the others. Casa Nova pecked everybody.

It was sad to say good-bye to all in "Solbakken."

On a cold morning in February I walked to the Borre station. Pius went with me for a bit of the way.

I was beginning my journey to Lima, found in the country called Peru—across the Atlantic, on the other side of South America. That was where all the members of the Kon-Tiki crew were meeting to build the raft that would take us from Peru to Polynesia.

The station master did not know where Lima was. "Where did you say you were going—to Lima? That must be in Sweden somewhere."

But he gave me a ticket to Oslo and that was the real start of my travels. I got into a train on the Vestfold Railway.

The railway was very old. It looked like this when I was a little boy—

—it looked like this when I went to Lima, and it will certainly look like this when I come back.

When I arrived in Oslo, I tried to insure my life for 50,000 kroner, but no one would do it. This is what the insurance agent looked like when I told him about the voyage I was going to take on a raft.

At 8 o'clock the next morning I was on board the ship *Lauritz Swenson*, bound for Panama!

And twenty-five days later I was taking a plane from Panama City, where the boat had docked, to Lima, Peru. From the plane, I could see brown rivers and a carpet of green jungle in Ecuador. I saw the corrugated iron roofs in Guayaquil glittering in the sun. I saw the moon shine over the desolate coastal desert of northern Peru, and at last Lima, like a brilliant jewel down in the darkness. The flight was over after eight hours and the great bird descended over the airfield of Lima, the capital of Peru.

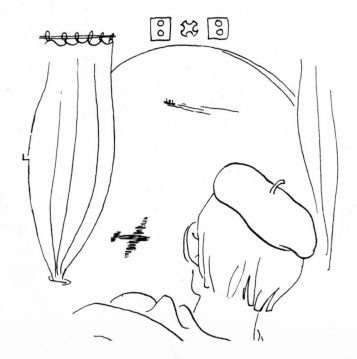

5

When I arrived, there were only two other members of the Kon-Tiki crew in Lima—Herman Watzinger and Bengt Emmerik Danielsson.

Apart from the president of Peru and some of the ministers, there were not many people who knew about our expedition or about the legend of Kon-Tiki. But soon all of Lima was to know, and then all of Peru.

The old town of Lima was founded by Pizarro in 1535.

Fifteen hundred years ago, however, there were many in Peru who knew of Kon-Tiki. According to Peruvian legend, he was the leader of a people who worshipped the sun, in fact Kon-Tiki himself was thought to be the son of the sun. But the city near Lake Titicaca in which Kon-Tiki and his people lived was attacked by other Peruvians, and it was destroyed. Kon-Tiki and some followers managed to escape to the coast, where they embarked on balsa-wood rafts and disappeared across the Pacific—to go home to the sun, the legend says.

This is *Machu-Pichu,* the site of the city built by Kon-Tiki's descendants.

Perhaps Kon-Tiki looked like

this   —or like this   —or like this.

These are all stone or clay faces that were dug up in South America.

1500 years passed without anyone giving another thought to this lost race, but then Thor Heyerdahl began to think about Kon-Tiki.

The Polynesians live on a number of small islands roughly in the middle of the Pacific Ocean, and no one is quite certain how they got there.

Thor also lived for a time on these islands, and while he was there, he heard talk about Tiki—one of the gods in Polynesian legend.

On some of the islands, Tiki was the most important god. It was said that he was son of the sun and that he had led his people out into the Pacific.

At last Thor Heyerdahl became so interested in the Polynesians that he devoted himself wholly to the study of where they came from. He worked at it for many years and came to the conclusion that the Polynesians had originated in South America and that Kon-Tiki of Peru and Tiki in Polynesia were the same person.

Kon-Tiki had gone home, not to the sun, but to Polynesia with his balsa rafts.

Thor Heyerdahl was so sure of his theory that he wrote a thesis about it. But no one would believe in his idea. No one would believe that a primitive balsa raft could carry men 4300 miles across the open sea.

"Then I'll prove that it's possible," said Thor Heyerdahl.

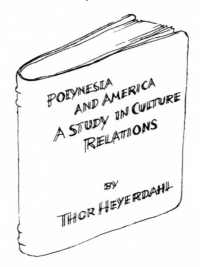

POLYNESIA AND AMERICA A STUDY IN CULTURE RELATIONS

BY

THOR HEYERDAHL

That was why we were at Lima—to build a raft of balsa wood like the ones in old Spanish drawings and cross the sea as we believed Kon-Tiki had done. The Humboldt Current, the South Equatorial Current, and the Southeast trade wind would help us to cross just as they had helped Kon-Tiki.

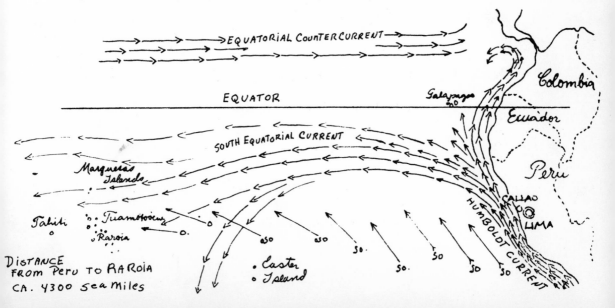

EQUATORIAL COUNTER CURRENT

EQUATOR

SOUTH EQUATORIAL CURRENT

Galapagos

Colombia

Ecuador

Peru

CALLAO
LIMA

HUMBOLDT CURRENT

Marquesas Islands

Tahiti

Tuamotou
Raroia

Easter Island

DISTANCE FROM PERU TO RAROIA
CA. 4300 sea miles

Shortly after I landed in Lima, the other members of the Kon-Tiki crew gathered. Here are the six men who were going to take this voyage halfway across the Pacific on a raft.

Knut Haugland
Herman Watzinger
Thor Heyerdahl
Bengt Emmerick Danielsson
Torstein Raaby
and I myself, who stands 6 feet 4 inches above sea level, am easily recognizable.

KNUT   HERMAN   THOR   JEG   BENGT   TORSTEIN

The Lima papers called us:

Los Expedicionarios
or
Los Tripulantes De La "Balsa"

Gerd Vold was secretary to the expedition. She looks something like this, but is much prettier. She gave us excellent help, and the papers called her the raft's godmother.

The first thing that had to be done was to get balsa logs for the raft.

Thor and Herman brought nine balsa logs from the jungle in Ecuador. Balsa is a kind of light wood, but it is not very

easy to cut. Nevertheless, they chopped down the trees themselves and brought them to a little stream which ran through
the jungle. There they tied the logs together with vines. Then
they sat on the top of the logs and drifted downstream all the
way to the port of Guayaquil in Equador. From Guayaquil, the
logs were sent by cargo boat to Callao, the port of Lima.

And now our work began.

The president of Peru gave us permission to build our raft
in the naval harbor.

He was also kind enough to lend us one of his cars.

There were a lot of kind people in Peru.

"*SKAAL, VIKINGOS DEL 'KON-TIKI'!*" they said. They liked
to have us around at their parties and they gave us a good
time. But that was not why we took three months to build
the raft. No, it was not so easy to build rafts in Peru.

We laid the nine logs side by side like organ pipes and
lashed each log to its neighbor with ordinary hemp ropes and
wooden pegs. We lashed a few smaller logs crossways on top
of the nine. This completed the hull.

We could not use iron in this vessel for nothing of the kind was known in the Americas before Columbus. On the top of the crosswise logs we laid half-rounded and braided bamboo as a kind of deck.

Then we built a cabin of bamboo and lattice work. The roof consisted of thin bamboo and banana leaves. It looked like it belonged in the middle of the jungle. Inside, it was not exactly a palace either.

13

The mast looked like this and was of mango wood, which is so heavy and hard that it sinks in water. We made a sail about thirteen feet by sixteen feet, and on it I painted the head of the god Kon-Tiki. At last the raft lay there completed, and it was such a strange craft that a crowd of people came to stare at it every day. It looked like a queer contraption lashed together with rope ends.

The old Spanish drawings we used as models were of bigger rafts than ours, but our raft was as exact a copy as possible.

But there were not many who believed things would go well for us, although we six did our best to believe it.

An admiral stood on board our vessel one day and shook his head. "You must be tired of life," he said. "These lashings will never hold in the continual motion out at sea. When three weeks have passed, I'll bet that you'll each be sitting on a log of your own and floating in all directions!" And he was so sure of it that he convinced a friend of his to bet a case of

whisky that this would happen. Well, we did not take the bet, for who would pay the admiral's friend a case of whisky if we went to the bottom?

All this was not exactly pleasant to hear. Later we got that case of whisky anyway!

It was much worse to listen to a fat little Norwegian skipper and his mate and boatswain than to an admiral and his friend. "The lashings won't hold," they said, "and if they *do* hold it'll take at least a year to get to Polynesia with this contraption."

"But there's another thing which is wrong," said the skipper, "and that's the balsa wood of the logs. Why, it's as porous as blotting paper. So when you're drifting west with the current, you'll soon find that the logs sink deeper and deeper . . ." and then he described how the water would rise above our ankles and up over our calves, and over our knees and stomachs—how the cabin would disappear and we would have the water up to our necks, yes, right up under our noses! I thought it sounded awful, for I am nearly a head taller than the others and if this happened I should be the last man. I already saw in my mind's eye only the tufts of my companions' hair and the fins of approaching sharks. Of Bengt Emmerik Danielsson I

16

did not see even a tuft of hair, for he had all his hair on his chin and was bald on the top of his head.

And there were those who maintained seriously that our feet would rot away. But luckily, we ourselves were so busy that we had no time to be afraid.

On April 27th the raft was christened with a coconut by Gerd Vold and received the name "Kon-Tiki." After the christening Gerd was given sunflowers by Thor.

We unfurled the sail so that the whole crowd could see the bearded face of Kon-Tiki, son of the sun. Speeches were made and the city and port had been decorated. Yes, there was a lot of life that day.

Our departure date was set for the 28th, and that afternoon Callao became black with people. Thor and a parrot stood on the nine logs, surrounded by journalists and farewell presents. The rest of us were expected any minute.

The tug that was going to tow us came chugging along, long before the agreed time. A party of sailors swarmed on board the Kon-Tiki and fastened the raft to the tug. Just at that moment the parrot escaped from its cage. Thor tried to stop the sailors and catch the bird at the same time. He only succeeded in doing the second and, amid tremendous cheering from the crowd, "La Balsa" began to move with Thor and the parrot and all the journalists on board. Thor's despairing cry "Los otros expedicionarios!" was drowned by the cheering, and it was not till well out in the harbor that the people in the tug understood that there was only one "expedicionario" on board.

When Bengt and I came down to the dock, we met people on their way home. A watchman at the gate stopped us and said that there was nothing more to see now. "La Balsa" had gone.

"But we're going to Polynesia with her," we said. Then he laughed loudly and barred the way still more firmly.

"But we are the steward and navigator," we said.

"And I'm the engineer," he said, with a wink. He was clearly a natural humorist. But we were not inclined towards humor just then; we pushed the watchman out of the way and hurried down to the raft's berth. There was nothing there but water and a few splinters of balsa wood. Then we saw the fair heads of Torstein and Knut in a boat with a load of people, and we jumped in on top.

Out in the harbor we caught sight of the Kon-Tiki's crossed mast with a mass of people under it. The first thing we did upon reaching the raft was to clear the deck of photographers and journalists.

In the middle of the heap we found Thor and the parrot, both severely battered by the Press.

All the ropes and woodwork creaked horribly while we were being towed.

A swarm of small boats followed us out, but when it grew dark, the small boats had to go home to bed. The next day we and the tug were alone, well beyond the island of San Lorenzo. Then the great moment came when we cut the rope which still fastened us to the tug. It was a strange sensation to see the tug disappear and to think of the enormous distance we were to drift on our little raft—a distance of open sea as far as from Boston to the North Pole and back again to Boston. And far, far out to sea, 4300 sea miles away, we were to strike a few small islands, as small as grains of sand, in a craft which couldn't be steered.

These thoughts came and went in my mind the first night on the open sea, while the Kon-Tiki tossed up and down and each log of the raft seemed to be going its own separate way. The log next to mine on which Bengt lay was behaving quite differently from the one on which I was stretched.

But on the morning watch the weather was fresh and fine. A feeling that we were beginning a new life filled us—a life shared with the sea.

We saw two cockroaches on the logs, and we sympathized with them. They were in the same situation as we were, but involuntarily. We called one Per and the other Lise.

Per was an unlucky fellow and tumbled overboard shortly after. But Lise was with us almost the whole way to Polynesia, until she perished in the same tragic manner. Our other fellow passengers—besides the parrot, Lorita—were about 1000 ants. They lived in a crossbeam under my pillow. And a few thousand barnacles held onto the underside of the logs.

An amusing group of passengers were a number of pelagic crabs in the tourist class. They joined us by jumping from the birds' feathers on which they were often sitting, drifting on

the sea, and then onto the Kon-Tiki. One of the crabs we called Johannes. He lived in a hole in a log aft and was more than willing to be fed scraps of biscuit. At last he became so accustomed to finding food outside his door that he no longer troubled to move. He grew fat and lazy, but went ashore in Polynesia. There he died, perhaps of hunger.

Fish were already jumping high around the vessel on our first days in the Humboldt Current.

But soon we had something else to think about. The sea and the wind were getting rough.

The third night was the worst—then we had a real struggle on the logs. The seas rose high over the stern, smashing against the steering oar and against the two men who were on watch there. The steering oar cracked even though it was made of tough wood as hard as iron. Our raft behaved well. The water poured over it continually. But that did not matter, for there were holes in the bottom so that the water ran out again just as quickly. The logs creaked and twisted, each in its own way. The cabin swayed in one direction and the mast in another, almost as if the whole raft were made of India rubber. But the lashings held well. The bad weather had more effect on us. Our bodies ached and we got little sleep. Knut lay flat and green with seasickness.

After the heavy sea, it became quite calm. All things have an end—and so the dirty weather stopped being dirty, and we felt that everything was very shipshape and pleasant.

The little cabin was better than the hotel in Lima, we thought. And here we did not need to put on ties for meals.

At one end of the cabin lay Herman, Thor, Bengt, and I. Knut lay at our feet, and at the other end lay Torstein with the radio and Lorita.

The Kon-Tiki's radio station was called LI2B, and was full of electric shocks. The rest of us took good care not to touch the operators, Torstein and Knut, without rubber gloves while they sat at the key. The dry batteries were continually getting wet and having to be changed.

One day we had a fright. A full-grown octopus waved all its arms close by the raft. We remembered that a fisherman in Peru had told us that large octopuses had a habit of embracing people.

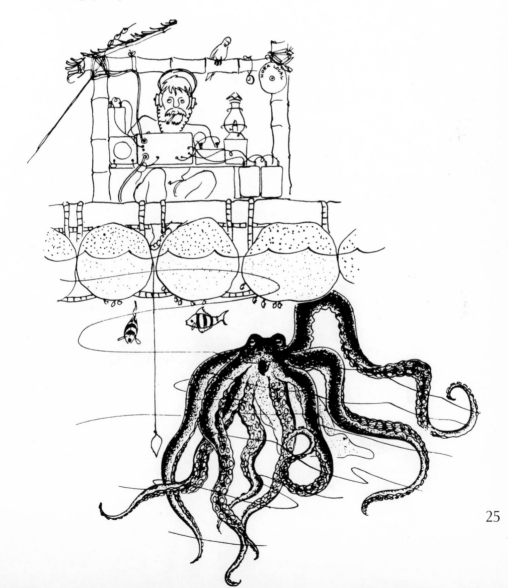

Luckily, the one we saw must not have cared for us, for it did not attempt anything of the kind.

After ten days the raft had drifted 500 sea miles in a north-westerly direction, through the cold, green water of the Humboldt Current and out into the ocean's warm, blue water.

And now the noblemen of the sea, the dolphins, flocked about us. The dolphin is both nice to look at and tasty to eat.

It is the swiftest fish in the sea too, for it lives on flying fish, so it has to be quick in its movements.

The dolphin shoots like a projectile from wave top to wave top and catches the flying fish when they come down into the water.

The dolphin can change color too—from deep blue to violet, red, yellow, and silvery white. They can be as long as five feet, and they liked puttering around the raft and rubbing themselves against the logs. There were so many dolphins around the raft all the time that we had only to fasten a hook to a stick, push the stick down into the school of fish, and haul up the best and biggest of them.

Flying fish came sailing through the air in swarms and smacked against the cabin wall. The cook's first job in the morning was to collect all the flying fish which had come on board during the night. One morning Herman found twenty-three. Once a flying fish almost hit the frying pan.

On one night a nasty snake-like fish jumped right in at the cabin door and right down into Torstein's sleeping bag! There was a scuffle in the dark. No one could find the lantern. First we would get hold of the snake-fish and then a man's leg.

At last we caught the fish. It was greyish-blue, about three feet long, and had teeth like a saw's. We tried to find out what

sort of a beast it was, but no description fitted it. So we put the fish into a tin of Formalin and took it with us to Polynesia. However, no one there could tell us what kind of fish it was either. We learned later that it was a *gempylus,* and that no one had ever seen a live gempylus before. Only skeletons of the fish had been found at one or two places in South America. So Torstein Raaby was presumably the first human being who had come in contact with a gempylus—especially in such an intimate manner, for it isn't every day that one has a gempylus in one's bed!

Near the Galapagos Islands, a big turtle came floundering up to us. It looked good and we thought of turtle soup. But the creature had no desire to become soup and paddled out of range as fast as possible.

There was no doubt now that we were going in the right direction. The southeast trade wind blew surely and steadily.

The Kon-Tiki kept up a good speed, sometimes as fast as two sea miles an hour. We determined this speed by throwing a chip of wood into the water ahead of us and looking at a watch to see how long it took our stern to reach the chip.

Once we were in the South Equatorial Current we kept a much higher speed. At noon every day the navigator—and that was I—drew a small circle on the chart, farther and farther away from South America. We could not do much to influence our course—the current and wind did that. We had only to fill the sail and keep the raft in her right position in relation to the seas. The cabin had only one opening and we had to have that on the lee side so that the seas would not come in. But very often the raft twisted around and the sail would kick like a wild horse. Then all hands had to come on deck to hold the sail and row the vessel around. This would take half an hour,

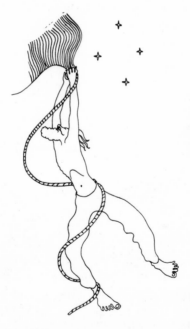

as she was quite heavy. Sometimes we had to turn out three or four times on a dark night to struggle with the oar and hang onto the sail under the stars. But we got accustomed to all this. Each man had two hours on watch and kept an eye on the course as well as he could, using an old boat's compass.

Time passed and beards grew, both on the raft and on ourselves. My beard was pleasant to scratch. It seemed to make me think so much better. Bengt had the biggest and most stylish beard of all—but on the top of his head there was not a single hair. His hair grew only under his chin.

Bengt's beard was chestnut-colored and of fine quality. The rest of us had different types of beards—highwayman, Francis Joseph, or just short and curly. But we had plenty to do in addition to scratching our beards, so the time did not pass slowly. The radio had to be looked after and repaired continually. Each man had his job to do on board besides his watch. When off duty we sat and talked, and if we did not do that, we just sat. Both the air and water were so pleasant and warm that we went quite naked. Down in the wide valley between the waves, so huge that they looked like hills on a landscape, it was very warm. But on the very top of a wandering water hill it was often so cold and windy that we had to put on some clothes again.

And, well, we fished—and it was no small fry we hauled up. Here is Herman with a tunny. It was so heavy that two men could barely carry it.

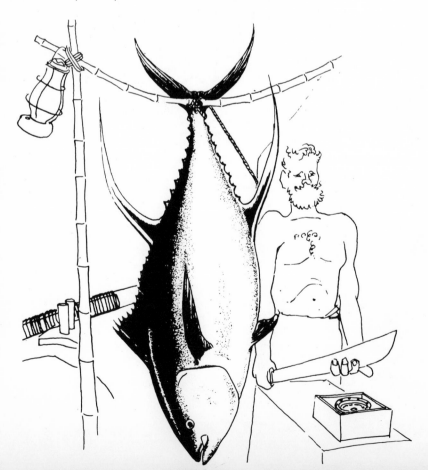

We saw swordfish too, but we did not catch any since they only go after swiftly-moving bait, and we couldn't manage that with our old tub. But we did catch sharks and plenty of them—twenty-eight in all. They are said to be greedy and strong, but easy to catch if the tackle is good. We had no proper shark hooks, only big cod hooks which we tied together and stuffed into a dolphin's stomach. We caught most of our sharks with this bait, actually pulling them onto the raft by their fins, when they came close enough. One morning, eleven brown sharks were prowling around us; we hauled up nine of them.

It was from the sharks that we got our pilot fish.

The shark has bad eyesight but it always has three or four little fish in attendance that signal it when something edible is in sight. As reward, the little pilot fish receive the scraps that fall from the shark's jaws.

When the pilot fish saw the very basis of their existence (the shark) disappear tail first up onto the raft, suddenly they found themselves unemployed and homeless. But then they apparently decided that the raft was a great big shark and they attached themselves to it. Since a lot of eatables came over the side of the Kon-Tiki, this made some sense. As we neared Polynesia the queer, flat raft-shark had at one time sixty to seventy pilot fish under the floor. We liked having the pilot fish and felt that they were our closest friends in the sea. Some of them swam 4000 miles on that occasion.

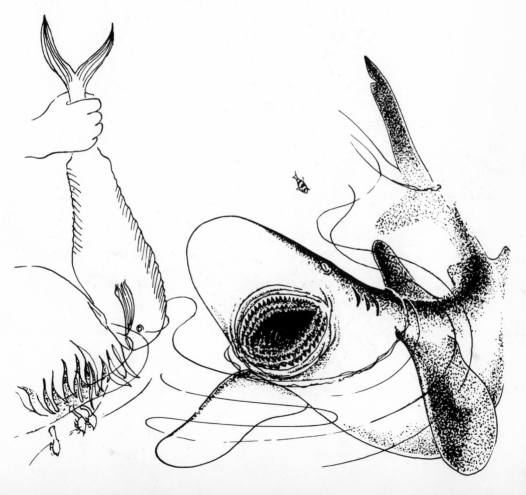

One day the world's biggest fish came and sniffed at the Kon-Tiki. That was a sight we shall never forget. It was as improbable as the tallest story.

If we had not seen the beast ourselves, we would have smiled indulgently at my drawing.

Knut was sitting washing his pants when the monster slowly bore down on him. Then Knut gave such a loud and hideous roar that the rest of us rushed up to see what was the matter with him. Then we roared just as loud, shrieking and laughing at the same time, the creature was so unbelievably huge and strange. The tension was unbearable—would the monster start chewing at the balsa or not? We realized that it was a whale shark, a very rare fish which can be sixty feet long and weigh fifteen tons and has 3000 teeth in its jaws. But this one was not quite as large—it looked as if it was about confirmation age. With a crowd of pilot fish ahead, he prowled around the raft, and he did this for so long that we plucked up courage. When he lay under the steering oar to scratch his back a bit, we thumped him in return, in a friendly way, to see how he took it. He liked it and came back to let himself be thumped three or four times. Then we gave him a bit of a jab with a harpoon, but we ought not to have done that, for he didn't like it and cleared off.

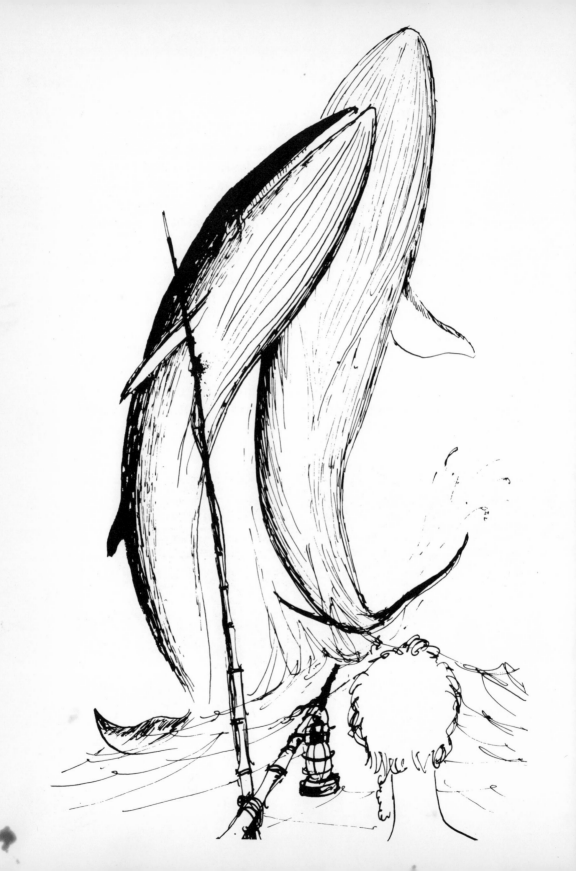

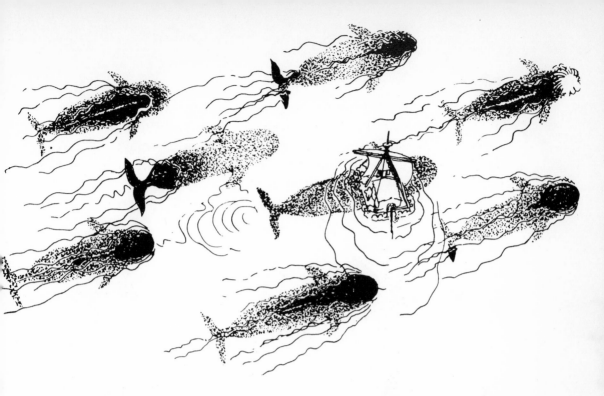

A day or two later we had a still bigger fright, for we came near to being capsized by whales, the giants of the sea. A large school of them bore straight down on our logs, blowing as they came. We lay there in the middle of the traffic and felt like a pushcart in New York City. And they didn't know anything about keeping to the right, either. Just as the blowhole of the first was on a level with our port mast, it dived under the raft with a gurgle, and the others did the same—luckily. We distinctly felt the backwash they made.

One remained lying under the raft for awhile and looked like a great black submerged rock.

Once Torstein and I saw two huge whales leap into the air and come smack down on the water with a tremendous splash. Then Torstein burst into roars of laughter, so unearthly that I was quite anxious about him.

It is curious to think that gigantic whales weighing up to 120 tons live on microscopic creatures. We caught these too. They are called plankton and are found in great quantities in all the seas. With the help of a small, bag-shaped, finely-meshed net we could get more than three pounds of plankton per hour in some places.

The mass of plankton looked like porridge—sometimes violet porridge and sometimes red porridge. Now and then we could make out the shape of individual creatures in the mass, such as the two I have drawn here. One is a tiny little crab; the other is, I don't know what—but it looked like an x-ray of itself.

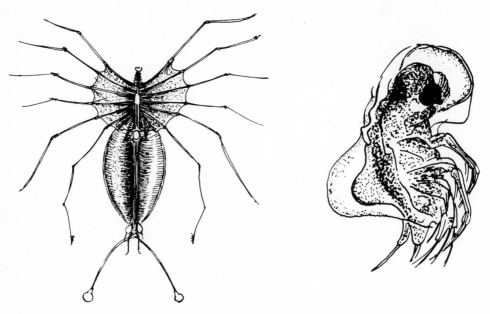

Then there was one which looked like a guitar with legs.

We tried to eat the plankton. It tasted like a mixture of stewed crab and wet paper, I thought.

We examined and collected in glass jars everything of zoological interest that we found. In order to be able to contemplate submarine life without interference from sharks, we rigged up a diving basket of bamboo and ropes. We wore goggles and sat in this as long as our breath lasted. With the goggles we could see as well underwater as above.

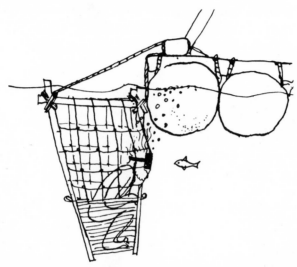

We had now been at sea nearly two months, and were more than halfway across. The wind was becoming more easterly. Each day carried us farther south, exactly as the current flowed.

All hands were in good fettle; no one had even had as much as a fishbone caught in his throat.

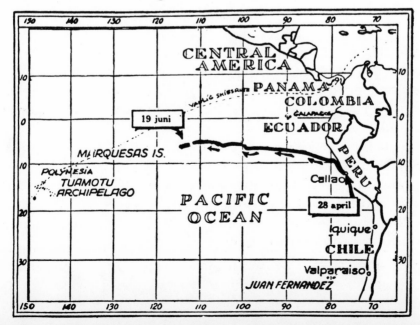

We never saw a ship, for there was no shipping in this area. We might have been on another globe, utterly remote from the world we knew.

Nor did we get bored with each other—on the contrary, we became like six brothers. If we felt an urge to be alone, we launched a small rubber boat which was attached by rope to the stern of the raft and floated in it until we wanted company again.

We had food enough—canned food and fish, coconuts, and groats. But some little black insects were living in the groats; they had been eating groats all the way from Peru. Steward Bengt separated them from the food, making two piles, and we took over for the insects.

We had brought drinking water from Peru in tins, and we collected rainwater. Now and then it rained so violently, that the air was as wet as the water. Then things would grow moldy and I got rheumatism in my right leg.

Otherwise the sun rose and set, and nothing changed except our position on the globe.

On June 28th, the sea washed over the logs and carried away Lorita, the parrot. We could do nothing to save her. She must have been drowned at once, poor thing. It was terribly sad, for we were all so fond of her.

A little later the same thing almost happened to one of our crew. A breeze caught Torstein's sleeping bag and blew it overboard. Herman tried to catch the bag, but made a false step, and he too tumbled into the sea. As the raft was making a good speed, it had passed before he could catch hold of it, and the steering oar was so covered with seaweed and so slippery that he did not get a grip on that either. The whole thing happened so quickly that none of us could help.

There he lay astern in the middle of the Pacific, thousands of miles from the nearest land. It was the worst thing that could have happened, for the raft could not turn back—that was absolutely impossible! We had to act quickly before the

sharks came. And Knut was the quickest. He flung out a lifebelt with a line, jumped into the sea, and swam back to
Herman with the lifebelt. He was just in time, for Herman was
already exhausted and a shark's fin was approaching. . . .

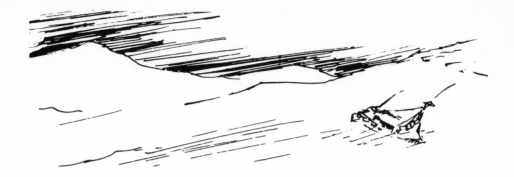

After this, we realized that to fall overboard was the most dangerous thing that could happen—that the Kon-Tiki could face storms and great beasts, but she could not pick up a man who lay in her wake. Henceforward, the man on watch was more carefully tethered to the vessel with a rope around his waist.

The weather was no longer as dependable. For a week the sail hung down slack and the heat troubled us quite a bit. Then came a small black cloud which grew bigger and bigger—and soon we were racing ahead into a storm, under bare poles.

Suddenly a wall of rain burst upon us and pressed the sea flat. Only the Kon-Tiki stood up against it like an old sodden barn in a meadow. No sooner was the tap turned off than the wind rose.

So it went on for many days. I only remember that my rheumatism was very active and that Herman crawled out with the anemometer from time to time and measured the speed of the wind at forty-five miles an hour.

But the Polynesian Islands were drawing steadily nearer. We were becoming anxious as to whether the Kon-Tiki would strike these small islands, or simply float by them. But the current took us as we had calculated—straight down to the densest part of the Tuamotu group of islands.

First we saw a solitary bird, and I am sure we never looked at a bird with greater interest. Then for a long time nothing happened, and we were getting tired of arguing as to who had seen the bird first, when a whole flock appeared.

And then one morning, after ninety-three days, we saw the easternmost of the Coral Islands, Puka Puka.

A low island lay to port, there was no doubt of that, and our reckoning said it was Puka Puka, so there was no doubt either that we had reached Polynesia.

But the Kon-Tiki just tumbled on westward with the wind and current and did not seem to care if there were ever so

many Puka Pukas in the neighborhood. She could not be maneuvered to the island and Puka Puka disappeared astern of us. But three days later we sighted another little coral island which was called Angatau.

We came so close to the island that we saw every coconut ashore, and got ready for stranding. But when there was only another fifty yards to go, the current carried us past the westernmost point and out to sea.

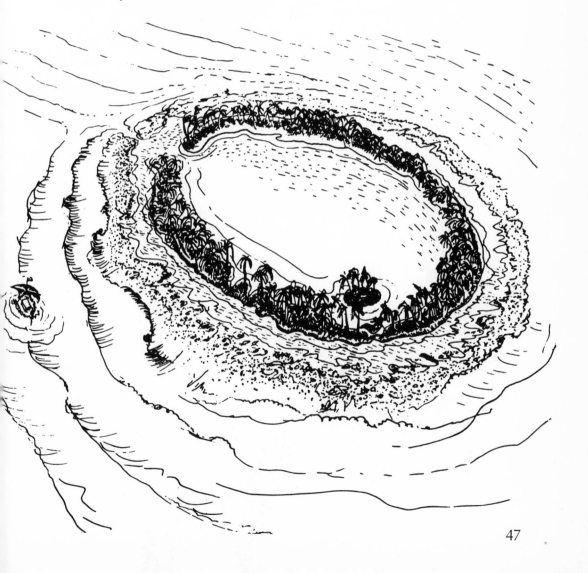

Just then a canoe came from the shore with two natives in it. "Good night," said one of them. "This is fine," we thought, "he speaks English," and we asked what the island was called.

"Good night," the native said again. Then Torstein asked him how his mother was. As the answer to this too was "Good night," we realized that he was not too strong in English. But there was no time for more conversation, for the raft was slipping on. We hauled down the sail and rowed with all our might with a few small paddles we had with us. The two natives helped, and still more canoes came and tried to tow the raft to shore. But the Kon-Tiki would not be moved—no, to Angatau she would not go, though we kept on rowing till nearly midnight.

Knut had gone ashore with the rubber boat to get more help, and he just managed to come aboard again before the light from the Kon-Tiki sank below the horizon to westward, so strong was the current.

Our situation was not bright. All around lay low, treacherous coral reefs, which could not be seen until one was quite close to them. The current and wind, too, were constantly changing in these waters—among the most dangerous in the whole world. There we lay in a craft which drifted along, following her own head, with no possibility of steering clear. On top of all this we had bad weather, with violent rain squalls and a northerly breeze.

But on the morning of August 7th, 101 days from Peru, the lookout shouted "Land ahead!" A look at the chart convinced us that it was Raroia, one of the larger islands. Soon we saw palms all along the horizon to the west, and we moved swiftly inshore towards them. Well, there was nothing else to do but to make ready for a landing in the midst of the breakers and coral reefs.

We hauled up the centerboard, lowered the sail, and packed away the things we thought were important in waterproof bags. We continued to do this until the noise of the breakers filled the air. Then it was time to put our lifebelts on our backs and our shoes on our feet.

The only chance we had was to be able to cling to the logs as long as our strength lasted, and hope that the Kon-Tiki would be flung upon the reef.

So we stood by.

It was a frightening sight, those breakers and reefs, and we were almost afraid we wouldn't make it. Before we had time to think any more about it, a sea came and heaved us right into the witch's cauldron. The raft gave a bump and a crack or two. Then we were drawn out again, as if to take off for the next jump. A green wall of water, as clear as glass, with snow on the top, rose behind us and the next minute rushed down and buried the Kon-Tiki and all on board. Finally the mast

51

snapped, the cabin collapsed, and there was a smashing and twisting and crashing. But we were all alive, squeezed under the bamboos or clinging tight to ropes. Several seas of the same kind came until what was left of the raft was halfway up the reef.

Then one by one we jumped down onto the red corals and ran in across the reef to safety. And after us came the raft, like a good-natured horse, with Thor and Torstein on its back. I can tell you that we were pleased with our raft. It had brought us to Polynesia with our lives and most of our equipment safe.

That Kon-Tiki, son of the sun, could have come to Polynesia in the same way, was quite certain.

We found the rubber boat far in on the reef. It was punctured, but we patched it and blew it up again for use in salvaging our things. About 600 yards away, on the edge of the reef, lay a small island. We put our log book, water tins, and provisions in the rubber boat and floated it to the island. We could not move a great deal that day, for we were all grazed and groggy. At last we could do no more, and we threw ourselves down on a green spot under the palms.

The island was so small that we could go around it in five minutes. There was no trace of people on it, nor on the neighboring islands either.

The first thing we had to do was to rig up a little radio transmitter which had been salvaged and tell the outside world that we were alive on an uninhabited island on the Raroia reef.

Just before we landed, Torstein had been in contact with a ham radio operator on Rarotonga and told him that if he did not hear from us within thirty-six hours he was to notify our contacts in the United States. When thirty-seven hours had passed the radio still would not work and we thought we could already hear the sound of aircraft in the distance. But suddenly we got an answer to our signals from an amateur in Colorado and from New Zealand, and we reported what had happened.

We waded to and fro between the raft and the island, collecting our things. It was then we saw this queer fat fish. When it was frightened it inflated itself to terrify its enemies by its appearance.

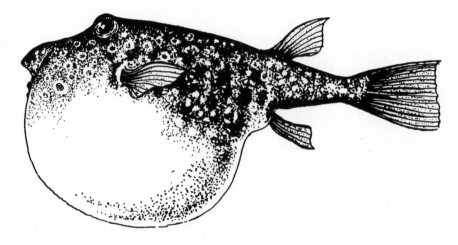

We saw a lot of snake-like creatures on the reef and in the lagoon as well. All over the place they lay in heaps and wriggled. We paid no particular attention to them as we tramped along. But later we heard that they were a very poisonous and fierce kind of snake-fish called *murena*.

After a few days of hard work we had settled pretty comfortably on the island with our private house and bathing beach. There was a garden with coconut palms and scented bushes. We thought this must be paradise and would have liked to have stayed there for a long time.

We dived in a lagoon that was full of submarine spectacles and saw a marvelously beautiful world. This drawing gives only a faint impression of it. There were corals which looked like petrified bunches of flowers, giant mussels with wavy mouths, and fantastic fish which exceeded anything the imagination could invent.

There were swarms of hermit crabs and robber crabs on the island. The hermit crabs were so easy to catch that a moderate-sized cooking pot became full in no time. They were as red as

cooked lobsters and as large as a man's fist. One night I awoke with one hermit crab sitting on my stomach and another on its way down into my sleeping bag. Yes, it was indeed a good place, we thought.

On the other side of the lagoon we could just see some other islands on the same reef.

After about a week had passed we saw a sail crossing the lagoon towards us. Through the binoculars we could see that there were two men approaching us in a sailing canoe. Thor took our flag and waved it. The two in the boat waved back.

When they waded ashore, they advanced with outstretched hands to show their friendliness. We said "Ia-ora-na," which means "good day" in Polynesian. Then they smiled and shouted "Ia-ora-na" in chorus. So now we were friends, and we said "Ia-ora-na" all that day and most of the next, for that was the only thing we could say in Polynesian.

Later another canoe came, and there was a chap in it who could talk a bit of French. We learned from him that there was a village on the other side of the lagoon, and that the people of the village had found a box floating in the water with "Kon-Tiki" written on it. This had puzzled them very much in the village, as Tiki was their old god. Someone had also seen a light at night on our side of the lagoon. But at last they had overcome their fear and here they were.

Bengt went back to the village with the natives, and the next day he returned with the chief himself, who was called Teka.

The chief was a smart fellow. He knew quite a lot and realized that we were not shipwrecked sailors, but a kind of expedition which had something to do with Tiki.

The chief brought with him the whole male population of the village. The men were tremendously interested in all the strange gear we had. They particularly thought the radio was great fun. And when Knut managed to get someone who was giving a talk, their jubilation was immense.

Then the whole crowd with the chief and ourselves at the head, waded out on the reef to see the strangest thing of all— our raft. They were greatly astonished and there was a lot more talk about Tiki. They pointed to the logs and the breakers and shook their heads.

The chief, Teka, wanted us to come over to his village as guests. We had no objections to this and set about moving our things across the lagoon in canoes.

While we were doing this, the water rose around the island and out on the reef the surf thundered as never before. It was too much for the raft too. It buffeted its way forward, making for the island, in a way it was a pleasure to look at. We stood by with ropes and caught hold of it. When it started to move out into the lagoon, we managed to fasten it to a palm trunk.

Over in the village there was an air of well-being. All who could walk or crawl had come to meet us. The women stood in readiness with wreaths of flowers and hung them around our necks.

We felt a bit embarrassed when they stuck flowers all over us—behind our ears and in our beards. But that is Polynesian custom, so there is nothing strange in it.

One of the ladies led us off to a hut and there lay a little boy who looked very ill. He had a nasty boil on his head. We understood that the lady was the boy's mother and wanted us to help him.

Knut had had some medical experience, and washed the boil with boric acid.

We put our medicine chest from the Kon-Tiki to good use, for there was neither doctor nor medicine on the island.

In the evening the Polynesians had a great feast at which we were guests of honor. While we sat and ate roast suckling pig, breadfruit, and chicken, the young girls danced around us. It was not the kind of dancing to which we were accustomed. No, they stood with their arms over their heads and wriggled their backsides rapidly.

When at last we had eaten our fill, the whole village sat down in a circle and the great dance began. Some of the natives played on a kind of guitar. And others sang. The music grew livelier and soon a young hula girl leapt into the ring in front of Herman. It was clear that she liked him and wanted him to dance with her.

At first Herman was not very happy about the idea. But she would not give way, and the rest of us teased him so long that he had no choice but to fling himself into a wild dance which left him quite breathless. We laughed till we were lying flat on our backs. But we ought not to have done so, for now one girl after another came and danced before each of us too.

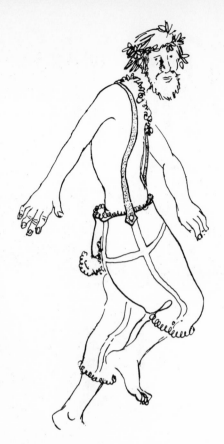

And of course we couldn't do less than Herman had. Even I, who was rheumatic and sat in my sheepskin trousers to warm up the rheumatism, had to step forward. I danced till my bones creaked and invented every step imaginable. It must have been very funny to watch, because there was a tear in the back of my skin trousers and a strip of skin with fur on it hung out, just like a rabbit's tail.

The people were doubled up and laughing till the tears streamed down their faces. Yes, there was a lot of fun over that hula dancing, and I am sure they still talk about it on Raroia.

They were a happy people of 127 souls, a few small black pigs, fowls, and dogs. They had no money, but used coconuts for barter. The coconuts hung in the palm trees and often tumbled down on the natives' heads, so that they may well be described as "hard" currency! In exchange for coconuts or copra, the islanders got anything they liked that was on board the trading schooners that visited Raroia twice a year.

Knut and Herman succeeded in curing the sick Polynesian boy with the help of the penicillin brought from the Kon-Tiki. They also radioed Los Angeles and consulted a doctor. All this made an enormous impression on the natives.

A few days before our departure we were ceremonially admitted into the tribe and received Polynesian names. Thor's name on Raroia is *Varoa Tikaroa;* Herman's is *Tupuhoe-Itetahua;* Bengt's is *Topakino;* Knut's is *Tefaunvi;* Torstein's is *Maroake,* and my name is *Tane-Matarau.* These were all names taken from Polynesian history and legend and are good names to have.

We learned by radio that the French Government schooner "Tamara" was on her way from Tahiti to fetch us on orders sent from Paris. And one day "Tamara" came with photographers and the administrator of the Tuamotu Islands on board. When the administrator saw the raft, he wanted to tow it right to Tahiti. It was a sad good-bye to the natives on Raroia. We had become fond of them and they of us.

The "Tamara" was quite an ordinary schooner with a motor which seemed to say "Papa, mamma, papa, mamma, papa, mamma, papa, mamma" all the way to Tahiti.

In Papeete there were celebrations and imitation hula girls with flowers. We planted a coconut which we had brought with us from Peru in the governor's garden. Today it has grown into a palm tree.

There is not much left of a South Seas' paradise in Papeete. There are big cars, movies, bars, galvanized iron, and chewing gum, but we enjoyed our visit. My rheumatism was worse though—so bad that I had to have treatment for it. I wondered if Kon-Tiki had got rheumatism too after his raft trip 1500 years ago!

There was only one person in Papeete who could cure my leg and that was Monsieur Milette. With massage and one thing and another, I was told he had cured many people who were much worse than I. Well, Monsieur Milette came. He

was a little, mild-mannered man with a curious long nose. He tackled the rheumatism with tremendous energy. But he did not want any money, he said. If I could help him to become a good clown for the Tahiti amateur competition, that would be payment enough for him. I felt this was a fair offer, so I accepted.

First he massaged me until I creaked, but that did no good. Then he tried electric shocks, but that did no good either. Then, he said, the only thing which will do any good is "Chinese nails," and he stuck some long silver nails into my leg at various "strategic" points. But the Chinese method, too, made me no better. Finally he pulled a canvas bag with a hole in it over my head and lit a fire under me. Then it was time

to make a clown of him. I gave him a longer nose, bushy eye-brows, and bigger ears. He borrowed my sheepskin trousers and went off to the competition.

Altogether there were three clowns competing. When Monsieur Milette saw them, he became so nervous that he couldn't say anything funny and unfortunately finished third. It wasn't my fault!

I still had my beard. It was a queer beard—like a kind of tri-color flag. Under my chin there was a red point, at the sides there were black curls, and under my nose was a straggly fair moustache which hung straight down, completely unheroic and impossible to make at all dashing. The others had been beardless for a long time. So I let mine go too—but in stages, to see how it set its stamp on a man.

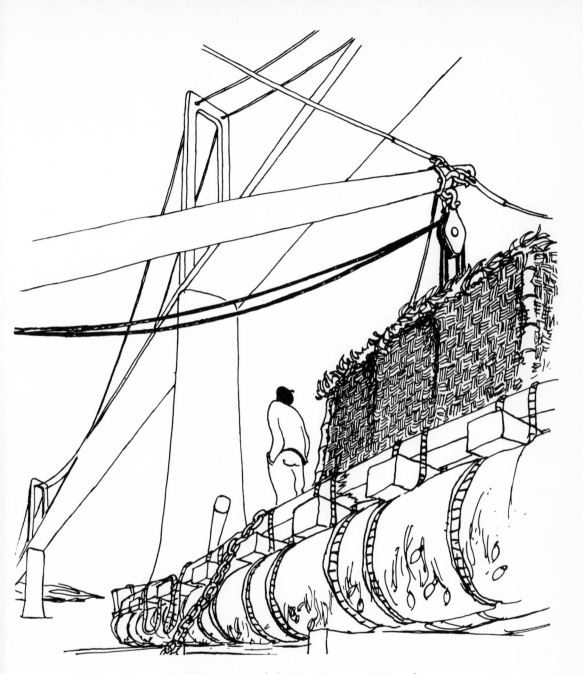

We were on Tahiti a good long time waiting for a passage to the United States. At last the ship "Thor I" came to Papeete especially to get us. The Kon-Tiki, too, was stowed on board the "Thor I" and after a voyage of ten days we passed the Golden Gate bridge into San Francisco.

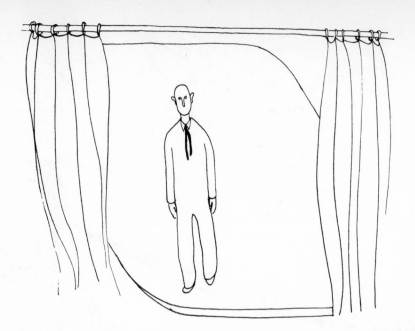

Here we said good-bye to brother Bengt, who was going to Seattle to study. He stood on the airfield, a lonely figure—without us, without hair, and without beard. His fine beard had been left on Raroia.

The Kon-Tiki lay in San Francisco harbor waiting for deck space to Norway, while we flew to Washington. We had a good deal of fun there, too.

The President invited us to visit him. When we arrived, he pointed to a globe and said, "That is where you sat on a raft for 101 days."

"Yes," we said.

"That's 100 days more than I'd have liked to sit on a raft!" said the President.

Then we flew home to Norway and I travelled by the old Vestfold Railway to Borre station. There stood Gundersen, the station master, and his wife and Anne Karin and several more. Anne Karin had grown so big. The cock and the hen were in glass bottles, and Pius had had a son. In the garden I saw the ends of both of them—and the end of my journey.